All about COMPOST

Recycling Household and Garden Waste

PAULINE PEARS

Revised by
CHARLOTTE GREEN

SEARCH PRESS

HDRA

Contents

Introduction

The natural world of lush vegetation and teeming wildlife has existed for aeons, without the intervention of the human race. It is a self-sustaining system – no one adds fertilisers to make plants grow, and no one has to come and take the rubbish away. No waste, no pollution.

The creatures that keep the system going are the myriad of tiny bacteria, fungi, insects etc., that consume and process plant and animal wastes. They recycle these wastes into a form that can be used to grow plants, and to feed animals that then defecate and die, continuing the cycle. These are the very creatures that recycle organic garden waste.

How did the bare tundra left by the receding ice-age come to be covered in forests, or the grey forbidding slopes of extinct volcanoes (even after fairly recent eruptions) turn into lush vegetation? Debris, dispersed by wind and birds, lodges in crevices and is slowly converted to soil which can support plant growth. Soon, living plants emerge, and the whole wondrous cycle begins. Even the indispensable sources of modern energy (oil, coal and gas) are the product of millennia of decomposed organic matter.

The twentieth century experienced an exploding world population and a revolution in chemical fertilisers, herbicides and pesticides. Modern agriculture demands ever-increasing levels of chemical use. In many cases, these practices have had devastating effects, as chemicals have allowed farmers to abandon the age-old practices of recycling organic matter, and crop rotation. Once-fertile soils have turned into dust bowls. Pests, which nature is perfectly capable of controlling itself, have become more prolific as the wildlife (which naturally keep pests and diseases under control) disappears with its dwindling habitats.

Organic farmers, who rely on recycling to maintain soil fertility and to keep pests and diseases at bay without the use of chemicals, are the exceptions to this rule.

Furthermore, the 'first world' has become a waste-producing society. In the UK, one person produces approximately 5kg (11lb) of waste per week (in the

Did you know?
It takes one hundred years to make 2.5cm (1in) of soil.

USA it is three times as much). Up to 50% of this waste is organic. The disposal of all this is a mammoth problem, and remains so despite the efforts of governments to reduce it.

Recycling and composting by everyone would greatly ease the problem. Now there are encouraging reports, from all over the world, about how the humble compost heap is making a real comeback. Some councils are allocating unused land round apartment blocks for tenants to grow vegetables organically. Some offer free compost or worm bins, and some make shredders available for hire at nominal sums.

By imitating nature, anyone can learn how easy it is to recycle waste and to grow natural, healthy food. If only in a small way, we can help redress the imbalance we have created in the environment.

This book is primarily aimed at people with small- or average-sized gardens and/or allotments; but the principles described apply equally to large farms and massive food-producing corporations.

Even people with no garden at all could consider adopting a worm bin. The resultant compost works wonders on house plants!

The book tells simply, with many colour illustrations, how to dispose of all your kitchen and garden waste, and how to put it to good use. It tells which wastes will compost, how that compost will make vegetables, flowers, trees and shrubs thrive, how it will help control weeds and pests, and how it will help save water. There is also a section on green manures for very keen gardeners. These are plants that can be grown to improve soil conditions.

The twentieth century hastily embraced chemicals as the answer to many of the world's problems. Perhaps, with your help, the twenty-first century will quickly return to natural ways.

Why recycle organic waste?

Grow healthy fruit and vegetables

It is easy to grow fruit and vegetables using only natural organic fertilisers and soil conditioners, such as compost and leaf mould. Chemicals fertilisers encourage sappy growth that is very attractive to pests and diseases. Organic materials produce sturdy plants that tend to be less prone to attack.

Encourage wildlife

Wildlife thrives where compost and other recycled materials are used as mulches and soil improvers. Small creatures, which in turn feed others, love the food and shelter that these materials offer.

Save money

Many local authorities charge for waste collection – a charge that is likely to increase. Even if you do not pay directly for waste collection, you will pay for it in taxes. By reducing waste, you will help to keep charges down. Furthermore, by making your own compost, you will save on buying expensive garden products.

Conserve water

Whilst the amount of waste generated throughout the world is on the increase, water is becoming scarcer due to greater demand and erratic rainfall. Compost retains moisture and reduces the need to water.

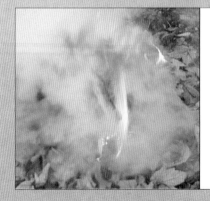

No bonfires

There is absolutely no need to have bonfires, which pollute the atmosphere and annoy neighbours. Most garden waste that is usually burned can easily be recycled into useful products. Bonfire smoke can be more harmful than smoking!

Grow flowers, trees and shrubs organically

Most plants and soils benefit from the addition of compost, leaf mould and other organic matter. It improves the soil structure, encourages good root growth, and provides food for the growing plants. Organic mulches can also help to control weeds.

Did you know?
Soil should never be left bare; it should always be covered with a mulch.

Alternatives to peat

The use of peat is causing the destruction of fragile peatland habitats and the rare plants and animals that live there. In the UK alone, 94% of peat bogs have been damaged or destroyed. Composted kitchen and garden waste is a wonderfully effective alternative.

Reduce landfill sites

Waste disposal throughout the world is an increasing problem. Landfill sites are unsightly and dangerous. Organic waste largely contributes to the build-up of dangerous gases in landfill sites. Composting your own organic waste will ease the problem.

Reduce pollution

Compost, leaf mould and other recycled materials can improve soil fertility, so chemical fertilisers, which can pollute rivers and underground water supplies, are not necessary. Compost can also help to reduce the use of pesticides – plants grown in compost tend to be more resistant to pests and diseases.

7

What you can compost

Anything that was once alive can be composted, though some items are best dealt with in other ways. Here are some common materials which, when mixed together, would make a good compost. Dead leaves can also be added to the compost or stored separately to make a leaf mould mulch (see page 32).

Note
Use only manures from vegetarian pets, such as rabbits and Guinea pigs. Cat and dog faeces contain dangerous pathogens which should not be put on the compost heap.

Did you know?
In many households, the organic waste is as much as 55%.

8

Farmyard manure

Pet manures and bedding

Stable manure and bedding

Deciduous hedge clippings

Wood ash

Conifer clippings

Natural fibre fabrics

Fruit skins

Vegetable peelings and kitchen scraps

Dead flowers

Coffee grounds

Citrus peel

Vegetable scraps and crop residues

Spent tea bags

Weeds

Nettles

Grass mowings

Torn paper and cardboard

What you cannot compost

Although approximately 95% of all waste can be recycled, the items shown on this page cannot be composted. Many local authorities have a recycling policy; some provide centralised banks for different materials, others actually collect sorted waste.

The following trash can be sorted and recycled:
- Magazines and large quantities of newspapers
- Glass bottles and jars
- Plastic bags and bottles
- Metal cans

Note

Return all unused medicines and pills to your pharmacist or doctor.

Check with your local authority about the disposal of other chemicals.

Do not buy spray cans if they contain CFC's.

Do not compost cat or dog faeces. These can contain dangerous pathogens.

Magazines and newspapers

Plastic bags

Plastic containers

Plastic wrap

Wire

Foam and plastic packaging

Disposable nappies

Coal ash

Glass bottles

Medicines and chemicals

Aluminium foil

Metal cans

Spray cans

Synthetic fabrics

Persistent and pernicious weeds

Persistent and pernicious weeds such as couch grass *(Agropyron repens)*, ground elder *(Aegopodium podagraria)* and bindweed *(Convuvulus arvensis)* can be composted. However, unless you can get your heap up to a very high temperature, the roots will survive. It is best to put these and other persistent weeds, which can choke vegetables and flowers, into an opaque plastic sack with no holes, where they will eventually rot down.

Cooked foods

Cooked foods can be composted, but avoid meat and fish which tend to attract rodents and flies. There are some special containers for disposing of meat and bones, but our tests showed that they were not ideal.

Did you know?
Recycling aluminium cans uses 95% less energy, and causes less pollution than making new ones.

Compost bins

Did you know?
Frequent turning of a compost heap ensures that the 'compost workers' never get short of oxygen.

Any organic matter just left lying around will decompose, but it is better to collect it together into a simple heap – cover it with an old carpet or plastic sheet and it will make good compost. Make the heap neater by using a compost bin. The following pages show you how to make various types of bin, and some examples of commercial containers. An ideal bin will have solid sides to retain heat and moisture and a cover to keep out rain. It should measure at least 90cm (30in) in each direction. Plastic compost containers should have a capacity of at least 250l (10ft^3). Choose a design to suit your garden.

Siting your bin

Site your bin on bare ground, somewhere convenient for emptying it and for putting the compost on the garden. You will probably want to hide it in a corner, but do not make it too difficult to get to or you will never use it. In a small garden you could grow a screen of plants to disguise it. Sooner or later, you must stop adding waste and allow what is there to decompose. This is something you should bear in mind when choosing a site. The simple answer is to have two or more containers or a sectional one such as the beehive bin (see pages 13 and 24–25).

Homemade bins

You do not have to be a particularly good handy person to construct a bin. Here are a few simple ideas for bins that are easy to build.

Carpet bin
A piece of old carpet wrapped round a circle of wire mesh will make an adequate container.

Recycling wooden pallets
Wooden pallets can be acquired quite easily from warehouses and storage depots, and these can be used to make very good compost bins. Three sides of this bin are formed from pallets nailed together. The insides are lined with netting and the gaps are stuffed with straw (newspaper, cardboard and hay could also be used). Two posts at the front hold loose wooden boards. These are added as the heap fills up, keeping everything neat and tidy. If you have enough space, make two bins, side by side, and you have your own version of the New Zealand box (see page 15).

Wooden box

You can either make a plain wooden box or obtain a wooden packing crate. Take out the floor and have a cover handy. This type of bin is easy to make and sturdy, but not quite so easy to empty!

Wooden 'beehive' bin

Sectional layers are made, with interlocking corners, and stacked as required. You can use different widths of wood for each layer. This type of bin makes it easy to turn a heap (see pages 24–25).

New Zealand box

This homemade version of a traditional compost bin is made using a strong static wooden box with a removable slatted wooden front.

Did you know?

The small black flies that may emerge when you lift the cover off a bin are fruit flies, and are quite harmless.

Post and wire bin

This bin is simple to construct. Staple double wire netting round four stout posts and stuff hay, straw, cardboard or newspaper between the wire. Two posts and a set of wooden slats in front would make it tidier.

Breeze block bin

Breeze blocks can make a very sturdy bin. Build up three sides with blocks, put two stakes in front and use wooden boards as a removable slatted front.

13

Allotment compost bins

Here are three ideas from the Maidstone and District Allotment Association. Most allotments are purely functional, so it does not really matter what the containers look like. The first is a pair of simple wire-mesh containers. The second is an old plastic water storage tank (drainage holes were drilled through the bottom), with a corrugated-iron enclosure behind it. The third is an old coal bunker with two openings at the base to shovel out the compost. It must have taken quite an effort to get it to the allotment! Note how they all have double bins.

Making a tyre bin

The disposal of old car tyres is a problem for modern society, and you will probably have seen mountains of them at some time. Fortunately, ways of recycling them commercially are being developed. You can also put a few tyres to good use by making sectional compost bins – old tyres are easy to obtain from almost any garage.

Use a sharp craft knife to cut round one wall of the tyre, half way between the tread and the wire rim (wetting the rubber with water will help). On the other side of the tyre cut round the wall, close to the tread.

①

②

③

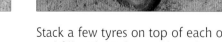
④

Turn the tyre inside out.

Stack a few tyres on top of each other and fill with kitchen and garden waste. Add more tyres as necessary.

Finally, cover and leave the contents to decompose.

Commercial containers

There are many different types of commercial compost containers available, some of which are shown here. When buying one of these, try to find one manufactured from recycled materials.

Did you know?
Some commercial containers are too tall for many people to use comfortably. Check the height before you buy one.

New Zealand box

A commercially manufactured double New Zealand box made from recycled wood. These are quite expensive but they do have all the features for making compost (see pages 24–25). They also solve the problem of what to do with waste when one bin is full.

Dustbin

Cut the bottom out of a large dustbin. You can make some air holes in the side, but this is not essential. If, like this one, it has tapered sides, turn it upside down.

Compost tumbler

A compost tumbler is designed to be turned every day. This regular mixing and aerating can make compost in three to four weeks.

Plastic containers

Some proprietry compost containers have a door at the bottom to allow the removal of compost. However, it is often easier just to lift the container off the heap.

15

Waste materials and how they compost

The following pages show readily available materials that can be used to make compost. They each vary in the way they behave in a compost heap. Soft young ingredients, such as grass mowings and young weeds, are quick to decay and help get the composting process started; animal urine is also a good 'activator'. Tougher materials, which rot slower, are also essential in a compost heap, as they provide the fibre which gives the compost 'body'. Without them the result will be a slimy mess. The key to success is to use a mixture of materials.

Activators are annotated with the symbol

Household

These two pages show how some common household wastes decompose. You will probably find many other materials that you can compost; remember everything organic (anything that was once alive) will decompose, though some items are best recycled in other ways.

Pet manures
Bedding from vegetarian pets such as rabbits, Guinea pigs, gerbils etc., contains a wide range of nutrients. This is very good for compost heaps, especially if bedding is straw.

Kitchen scraps (including food leftovers)
These make a good addition to the heap, especially when mixed with other ingredients. It is best to exclude meat and fish scraps, as these can attract flies and larger creatures.

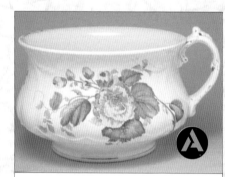

Urine
Urine, both human and animal, is a wonderful source of nitrogen and potassium. It can be diluted and then watered on to a compost heap. However, too much added to a heap will raise salt levels and inhibit worms.

Paper and cardboard

Torn and scrunched up, or shredded, paper can be composted – in fact, soiled paper towels and tissues are excellent ingredients for the compost heap. Large quantities of paper, however, are best put aside for recycling in other ways, or used with compost/mulches for weed control (see pages 30–31).

Cardboard can also be added to a heap if it is torn up and mixed in well. Tough cardboard is best sent for recycling, or used for lining compost bins (see pages 12–13).

Tea and coffee

Tea leaves, tea bags and coffee grounds are all good additions to the compost heap.

Eggshells

These do not compost quickly, but can be added to the heap.

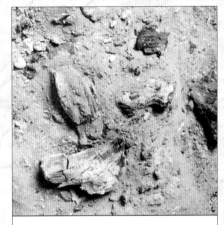

Wood ash

Wood ash provides potassium and lime. Do not use coal or other ashes.

Fabrics

Natural fibre fabrics will add bulk to compost. Do not add synthetic fabrics. Wool is a good source of nitrogen.

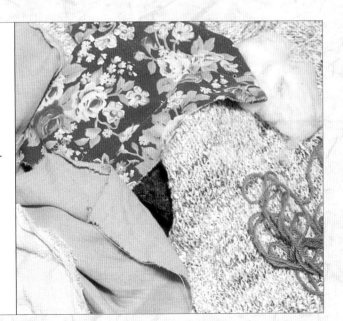

Hair

Human and animal hair contain good levels of nitrogen. Moisten well when adding to the heap. Hair takes a long time to decompose.

Garden

Even a small garden can produce an extraordinary amount of compostible materials, especially in autumn. Never throw anything away, as it can all be composted and put back into the ground.

Vegetable crop residues
These are good compost ingredients. Crop residues will vary in the rate at which they decay, depending on age. Tough items are best chopped up before composting.

Brassica stems
Stalks, stems and leaves of cabbages, sprouts and other brassicas can be quite tough and slow to compost. Chop them with a spade or put them through a shredder to speed up the process. Alternatively add to a compost trench (see page 23). Do not add roots if infected with clubroot.

Rhubarb leaves
Although poisonous to eat, these leaves are quite safe to add to a compost heap.

Potato haulm
Blight-infected haulm can be composted in a hot heap. Blight-infected tubers should not be composted, as they will spread the disease if they grow again the following year.

Diseased plant material
The intense biological activity in an active compost heap should deal with most plant diseases. However, it would be wise to omit plants infected with diseases such as white rot, clubroot and tobacco mosaic virus, as these can survive harsh conditions. If a compost bin is filled slowly, a little at a time, it would also be inadvisable to add plants with diseases that survive in dead or decaying plant material – mildews, grey moulds and foot rot, for example.

Weeds
Most weeds are good for the compost heap. Weed seeds will be killed in a hot heap. Otherwise, avoid adding seeds or simply hoe off any weeds that grow from the compost. Persistent perennial weeds are best killed off before being composted (see page 11).

18

Hedge clippings and prunings

Soft and young clippings can be added to a compost heap together with everything else. Shred longer clippings to help their decay.

Woodier prunings and clippings will take longer to rot down – beware of thorns as they can take years to decay. Small quantities of woody clippings can be composted as usual, but larger volumes may be best dealt with in a separate heap. Shred or chop them up as much as possible, mix them with grass mowings, chopped nettles or another activator, put everything in a compost bin and water well. Comfrey or nettle liquid can be watered on these prunings instead of mixing them with grass. The heap is likely to heat up, darkening the prunings. After a few months, these can be used as a mulch on perennial beds and paths.

Evergreen clippings such as laurel, holly, cuppressus and other conifers may tend to make a more acid mulch.

Autumn leaves

Small quantities of leaves may be added to a heap. Being old and tough, they are a useful balance where grass mowings and kitchen waste are the main ingredients. Store them in black plastic sacks until needed. Large quantities are best made into leaf mould (see pages 32–33).

Nettles

Every gardener should keep a clump of nettles. Not only are they good for wildlife, but cuttings mixed into a compost heap will help to start the composting process.

Comfrey leaves

These are quick to decay and they provide a good source of nitrogen and potassium. They will help heat up the compost heap. See also page 40.

Grass mowings

These heat up rapidly as they rot. They need to be well mixed with tougher, more fibrous materials to make a good compost. Too many will make a smelly, slimy heap.

Farms and smallholdings

Animal manures are a rich additional source of nutrients that will supplement recycled garden waste. They are usually available mixed with straw bedding; chicken and pigeon manures, which are very dry, may be available neat. If you do not have your own supply, bags or sacks of it can easily be purchased (some people give it away). However, avoid buying manure from intensive farms where animals are kept in unacceptable conditions, and where growth promoters and other chemicals may be used. Avoid fresh hay and straw that has been sprayed with herbicides, as this may distort the growth of tomatoes and cucumbers.

Did you know?
You can teach pigs to defecate in the same place every day.

Cow manure
This is an excellent source of all nutrients. It is usually available mixed with straw. It can be composted separately or mixed with both kitchen and garden waste.

Hay
Old and spoiled hay can be added to a compost heap. It also makes a good, rich mulch around fruit trees and bushes, providing food and retaining moisture in the soil.

Poultry manures
Manure from chickens, ducks, geese, pigeons etc., can all be used. They are all rich in nitrogen, and are excellent for 'activating' a heap which has a lot of tough material in it.

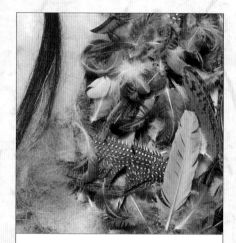

Feathers
These contain readily available nitrogen. Use them sparingly.

Straw
Old, spoiled straw is best for a compost heap. It is a useful balance where kitchen scraps and grass mowings are plentiful.

Pig manure
These young free-range pigs spend some of their time in a large barn. Their bedding is excellent for the compost heap.

Sheep manure
This is one of the best and most highly concentrated manures. It is not easy to acquire, except at lambing time when some sheep come indoors.

Horse, pony and donkey bedding
This contains many nutrients. If the bedding contains wood shavings or sawdust, the manure is best composted separately and then used as a mulch on perennial beds.

How to make compost

Did you know?
You should place a compost bin on to soil rather than on a hard surface. Soil will allow drainage and easy access for worms.

Many people are put off from making compost, either because they believe it to be dirty and smelly or because it is too scientific for them. Both beliefs are 'rubbish'.

Composting is fired by a natural process – the feeding of countless natural microbes, fungi and other creatures that appear as soon as a compost heap is started. We cannot stop things from rotting down. However, these creatures do need a balanced diet (see page 16) to create good compost.

There are many ways of making compost successfully; the important thing is to choose a method that suits you and your garden. The quickest way is to process lots of different types of waste at once (see pages 24–25). Many households, however, do not generate a lot of waste so, fortunately, there other ways of making good compost.

The bit-by-bit heap

If your natural waste is limited to kitchen scraps, grass mowings and some weeds, you can still make a good compost by mixing them with scrunched-up household paper waste. Paper towels, egg boxes, cardboard boxes and tubes, old newspapers etc., can all be used to add air and 'body' to the heap. In fact, any paper waste that appears in the kitchen can be added to the vegetable scrap container. Ideally, mix paper and vegetable waste in equal volumes. Do not overdo the paper; large quantities of newspapers, for example, are best taken for recycling.

Worm composting

If kitchen waste is the only ingredient available for composting, consider using a worm composting system (see page 28).

A bit-by-bit heap in a commercial, plastic compost bin. The ingredients – kitchen scraps and scrunched-up paper, with a few weeds and leaves – are left to decompose without turning the heap.

Did you know?
Woodlice are welcome visitors to your compost heap.

The compost trench

If you have relatively little kitchen and garden waste, it can still be put to good use by burying it in a hole or trench in the garden. This is a good method for the winter months, when there is little other plant material available to compost. When the trench is full, leave it to settle for a few weeks and then plant over it. Runner beans, pumpkins and courgettes love the moist rich conditions that trenching provides.

Dig a trench about 50–75cm (20–30in) deep and start to put your waste materials at one end.

Cover the waste with soil.

Add more materials and cover them. Continue until the trench is complete.

When do I stop adding to the heap?

The materials in a compost bin shrink as they decay, so it could take a long time to fill the bin completely.

If you use lots of mixed materials, and make an all-in-one heap, just leave it until the compost is ready.

On the other hand, if you add small quantities of waste, bit by bit, you will have to decide when to call it a day. Once or twice a year, remove the container from the heap and look at what you have got. There should be finished compost at the bottom, grading up to unrotted material at the top. Separate and use the compost, put the unfinished material back into the bin and start again. Alternatively, cover the maturing heap with a sheet of black plastic and leave it to compost completely.

When is compost ready to use?

Your compost will be ready to use when the majority of the original ingredients are no longer recognisable. This may take as little as three months, or as long as a year, depending on the ingredients and the composting method. Within reason, the longer you leave it, the finer it will be. However, compost will still be worth using whether it is fine and crumbly, or lumpy and stringy.

> **Did you know?**
> Tiny, creamy-white, jumping creatures found in compost are called springtails. They are harmless and recycle vegetable matter.

Do compost heaps attract pests?

Beginners are often concerned that a compost heap is a breeding ground for pests and diseases. Compost heaps are full of microorganisms, and larger creatures, but they are simply doing their job, and are not going to infest your garden.

Tiny black fruit flies may appear in summer, especially from heaps that are rich in kitchen waste. These can be annoying, but are quite harmless.

Larger houseflies are only a problem if meat scraps are added to the heap.

23

Making quick compost

If you are a keen gardener, here is a way to make compost quickly and efficiently. You may only achieve this sort of heap occasionally, but it is very satisfying when you do. Bringing in materials such as manure and autumn leaves can bulk up garden waste. The homemade, sectional wooden 'beehive' compost bin shown on page 13 is ideal for this method.

compost bin shown on page 13 is ideal for this method.

Did you know?
The ideal compost heap should keep rain out and keep heat in.

For really quick compost, the aim is to fill a compost bin in one go. Collect together all possible ingredients over a period of a week or two. Mow the lawn, trim the hedge, weed the border and so on. If possible, bring in a sack or two of manure, and do not forget the leaves collected in autumn. Remember the importance of a good mixture – soft sappy stuff to get the heap going and tougher, more fibrous, materials to give a good end product.

Chop chunky, tough materials with a sharp spade, or put them through a shredder. This will help speed up the rate of decomposition dramatically.

Thoroughly mix all the ingredients together, combining the soft with the tougher, more open ones.

Start to pile everything into the bin. Spread each layer evenly and gently firm them down.

Water dry ingredients as each layer is added.

Add more sections of the bin as the heap gets bigger.

7. Cover the heap with a sheet of plastic and a piece of old carpet to retain heat and moisture and to keep the rain out.

The composting process will soon start and the heap will heat up. To help speed things up, turn and mix the heap as often as possible. The design of the beehive bin helps you perform this task easily and effectively. Apply more water if the material is dry, or add more dry ingredients if it is too wet.

Did you know?
If you put a lot of citrus peel into the heap, harmless, white, threadlike worms can appear in large quantities.

When the compost is ready (see page 23), remove it from the container and start again.

Note
A container can be removed from a maturing heap if you then cover the heap with black plastic and/or old carpet until the compost is ready.

Composting in hot and cold climates

Did you know?
There are more bacteria in a teaspoon of soil than there are people on our planet.

Composting methods, whether in the tropics or in areas of extreme cold, essentially remain the same. However, there are some differences, especially in tropical areas of the world.

Extreme heat

All composting processes are accelerated in hot conditions. However, hot tropical areas have problems with moisture – it either does not rain at all, or it falls in torrents.

During the dry seasons, composting in a pit or hole in the ground helps retain moisture. The waste materials are covered with a layer of soil or thick leaves and left to rot down.

Heaps are also made above ground and covered with large, thick leaves when heavy rains are expected. Torrential rain could leach out much of the compost's goodness.

In parts of Africa, the 'improved cattle enclosure' method is used. Crop residues are heaped into a cattle enclosure (very often housing just one or two cows). What is not eaten by the animals is trampled and mixed with the dung and urine. The result is an excellent fertile mix for crops and vegetables.

A tropical compost heap being covered with large leaves to keep the heat in and rainfall out.

This African mother used to go to market and divide her money between chemical fertilisers and extra vegetables for her family. Then she learned about natural compost. In these two pictures she shows the difference between maize grown with chemicals (right) and maize grown with compost (far right).

26

Pit composting being demonstrated to African villagers.

This typical African vegetable and flower garden is fertilised solely with compost.

Extreme cold

In some countries it can be extremely cold in winter and the composting process almost comes to a halt. Here, an indoor worm bin is a good alternative to an outside heap. In rural areas, food for wildlife is scarce, so watch out for marauding animals such as bears or raccoons, unless you do not mind having your trash scattered everywhere. Special raccoon-proof compost bins can be purchased in North America.

Worms that gobble waste

If the main compostible material you produce is vegetable and kitchen waste, then you might consider acquiring a worm bin and practising what is sometimes called vermiculture. A worm bin provides a far more effective way of recycling small quantities of waste than a traditional compost bin. If managed properly, a worm bin will be odourless, yet it will dispose of all your kitchen scraps, plus some garden waste. Worm casts, as this material is called, make a valuable, high-quality compost.

This inspiring story comes from the World Resource Foundation. An Austrailian vineyard composted the organic waste from grape-processing with worms. The product was added to the vines under a straw mulch and showed an increased grape yield of up to 50% in a single season.

Worms

The obliging 'animals' who chomp their way through almost any organic waste are called brandling worms, *Eisenia foetida*. They are buff/red-striped, hence their common name, tiger worms. Unlike the common earthworms that live in soil, brandling worms can be found naturally in any decaying organic matter, piles of leaves and in compost and manure heaps. They can also be purchased from fishing tackle shops, which sell them as bait, or by mail order. Ideally, it is best to start a worm bin with about one thousand worms – about 500g (1lb) in weight. If a smaller quantity is used at the start, the process will take longer to get going.

Worms need to be kept in a container that provides dark moist conditions; there is no need to make it 'worm-proof' as the worms will stay where they are happy. They work best at temperatures between 12–25°C (55–75°F), but they will still be active, albeit slower, in cooler conditions. They dislike being too hot.

Brandling or tiger worms.

Soil-living earthworms.

Brandling worms produce cocoons, each containing several eggs.

One brandling worm can produce fifteen-hundred offspring in a few months, so numbers will soon build up, and you may have some to give away.

Homes for worms

A simple, plastic dustbin can easily be converted into a worm bin. The drawing opposite shows you how to set one up.

Feeding your worms

Worms will make compost from any form of vegetable waste. Chop large pieces to give them a start, and add torn up news-paper to soak up any liquid. How fast they process the waste depends on the number of worms and how warm it is. The rule is 'little and often', adding another batch of scraps when the previous helping is well colonised by working worms. If you add more than they can cope with, the scraps will start to putrify and smell. With a new worm bin, start feeding slowly, and gradually build up the quantity added as the worms multiply. Add the food to the surface of the bedding or compost, and keep it covered with a damp newspaper. Worms can manage for weeks without additional food so there is no need to engage a 'worm-sitter' when you go on holiday!

Empty the bin once or twice a year, or more often if it fills up. Scoop off the top layer of worms and uncomposted waste and set aside. Remove the composted material, replace the worms and waste, and start the system off again. It is best to do this in the spring or summer, so that the bin is beginning to fill up again when the cold weather comes.

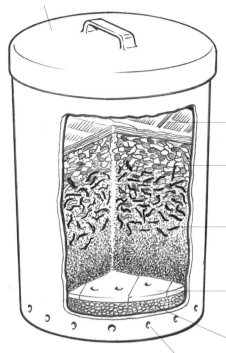

Put a lid on the bin

Cover the waste with newspapers to keep it damp

Add a little chopped kitchen waste

Start the worms off in a moist bedding – shredded card or paper, leaf mould or compost

Place a board, drilled with a few small drainage holes, on top of the gravel

Put a layer of gravel in the bottom of the bin

Drill a few holes near the bottom of the bin to let liquid escape

There are several commercial worm bins available. This one is particularly good for extracting finished compost.

Problem-solving

If the contents of your worm bin start to smell, the worms are not processing the waste fast enough. This can be due to:

- Too much waste for worms to digest – reduce the addition of waste until the colony has increased.

- Temperature too low or too high – move the bin to a more suitable location.

- Contents too wet – do not add any liquid with the waste material. Drain off liquid from the bottom of the bin. Mix in scrunched up or shredded newspaper.

- Contents are too acidic – cut down the addition of citrus peel. Dust the surface with a handful of calcified seaweed.

29

How to use compost

Compost is a valuable soil improver that can be used almost anywhere in the garden. It supplies plant foods, including trace elements, in a slow-release form. Compost will also improve the soil structure – light, sandy soils are able to hold on to more water and plant foods, while heavy soils will drain more freely and release the plant foods they contain. There is evidence to show that compost can also help to control soilborne pests and diseases, and that compost-grown plants are less attractive to pests.

Did you know?
Vegetables such as peas and beans make nitrogen fertiliser out of the air and store it in their roots.

How to apply

Compost, both garden and worm, can be applied as a surface mulch or incorporated into the top 15–20cm (6–8in) of soil. It can also be used as a top dressing for tubs and planters, and mixed with proprietary potting composts to make them richer. Worm compost tends to be richer, and quicker acting, than garden compost.

Apply compost to the soil during spring and summer to make best use of the plant foods it contains.

How much and where

How much compost you use depends on the plants you are growing and the current fertility of the soil. The maximum recommended annual rate is one wheelbarrow load per 5m^2/yd^2. Use this for greedy feeders, such as potatoes, blackcurrants and roses. Brassicas (the cabbage family) also thrive on a well-composted soil.

If you use a four-year rotation in the vegetable plot, well-rotted manure or compost on the potato/tomato bed, and compost on the brassica patch, should provide sufficient feeding.

Fruit, other than blackcurrants, should only need a mulch of compost every four or five years, with other less rich mulches, such as leaf mould, applied in the intervening years.

Most shrubs should not need the richness of compost, but they do appreciate a mulch of some sort. Herbs, in the main, do best in dry, poor soil, but mint, chives and parsley will benefit from a dose of compost.

A wheelbarrowful of compost can be used on about 5m^2/yd^2 of ground. This picture shows a marked-out plot on a raised bed, approximately 1.25m (4ft) wide.

Tomatoes and chard

Tomatoes thrive in a well-composted soil. Chard also appreciates moist conditions.

Brassicas

Brassicas – members of the cabbage family – do best on fairly rich soil. Apply compost before planting, or later as a mulch. Overwintering broccoli, kale, etc., may also benefit from summer mulch.

Curcurbits

Courgettes and zucchinis can be grown directly on the compost heap. Also shown here is the spaghetti plant, an unusual member of the family which also includes cucumbers, marrows, pumpkins, squashes etc.

Flowers

Roses that are pruned hard every year benefit from compost mulch. The young rose bush (far right) is *Rosa* Kent. Although most annuals do not require a lot of compost, French marigolds do enjoy a rich soil.

How to make and use leaf mould

Wherever deciduous trees grow, autumn is intensely evocative and picturesque with its hues of yellow, orange, red and brown. In the end, however, there are carpets of leaves on the ground. Many gardeners still burn them. This practice has now been banned in many countries but, even where it is not, remember that fires do cause pollution, and they are definitely not 'neighbour friendly'.

Most of these leaves have to be gathered up anyway, so why not just put them straight into a container and leave them to rot down into leaf mould? A simple wire mesh enclosure or a black plastic sack will do fine. Leaves are very slow to rot if dry, so collect them after it has rained or water them well as you fill the container.

Some leaves can be added to a compost heap, where they are useful to balance lots of kitchen waste and grass mowings. Keep a few full sacks next to the heap for the following season. Large quantities are best dealt with separately.

Leaf mould can be used on the soil in almost any part of the garden. Its main effect is to improve the physical structure of the soil, which in turn makes the soil more fertile. It can be used as a weed-supressing and moisture-retaining mulch, dug in, spread over a lawn, sprinkled over seeds or for making potting compost (see page 39).

Leaves take a year or two to decompose to a usable form (they do not have to be completely rotted through). To speed up the process, mix grass mowings in with the leaves next season. This makes a richer leaf mould, and is a good way of using up excess mowings.

Leaf collector
If you can afford it, this leaf collector finely chops the leaves and even chips small branches. The resultant mix can be used directly on the garden, or added to the compost heap.

Plastic sack
Leaves will decompose in a plastic sack. Tie the top of the sack loosely to make a neat bundle.

Wire mesh container
A simple wire mesh container can be constructed for making leaf mould.

Leaf mould for flower beds

Leaf mould makes a good mulch on all flower beds. It looks good and helps keep the soil moist.

Leafmould with strawberries

Strawberries do not like too rich a soil. However, a good leaf mould mulch is beneficial – it helps retain moisture.

Sinapis alba
MUSTARD

Annual • Tender • Height 30–60cm (12–24in)

Sow in late spring to late summer. Grow for up to eight weeks. Matures very quickly in warm weather (one of the quickest growing green manures). Once yellow flowers form it gets tough quickly. Susceptible to clubroot. Can be used in salads and the seeds for making mustard.

Trifolium incarnatum
CLOVER, CRIMSON

Annual • Semi-hardy • Height 60cm (24in)

A vigorous quick-growing clover with wonderful red flowers which bees love. Sow in late spring and summer. Grow for two or three months in summer; may over-winter from an autumn sowing. Prefers a light soil. Nitrogen fixing.

Trifolium spp
CLOVER, RED AND ALSIKE

Perennial • Hardy • Height 30cm (12in)

Similar plants – one with white flowers, the other red ones – much loved by bees. Red clover is more bushy and deep rooting. Sow in late spring and summer. Grow for a few months, or for up to two years. Cut down after flowering to encourage new growth. Prone to drought. Nitrogen fixing.

Trigonella foenum graecum
FENUGREEK

Annual • Semi-hardy • Height 60cm (24in)

An attractive quick-growing, bushy plant with insignificant white flowers and a mass of foliage. Likes heavy but well-drained soils. Sow in late spring and summer. Grow for up to three months.

Vicia faba
BEAN, WINTER FIELD

Annual • Hardy • Height 90cm (36in)

An agricultural variety of the broad bean, usually grown for animal feed. Sow in autumn. Grow over winter. Can be cut down and left to regrow once – a useful trick if plants have toughened.

Vicia sativa
TARES, WINTER

Annual • Hardy • Height 75cm (30in)

A rapid-growing, bushy vetch which controls weeds well once established. Sow in spring or late summer. Grow for two to three months, or over winter from a late sowing. Likes heavy, alkaline soils but cannot stand drought. Can be mixed with grazing rye. Provides a good supply of nitrogen for a following crop such as cabbages or other leafy vegetables.

Other ways to recycle household waste

Something like 95% of all the waste generated by our homes and gardens could be recycled commercially. This book has shown how you can deal with nearly half of this waste which is organic. The rest – plastic, glass, metal etc. – can all be taken to recycling centres (some areas may have special bins for these). However, you can put quite a number of 'throwaways' to good use in both your home and garden. The suggestions shown here are practical and attractive. Doubtless you will know or come up with many more ideas of your own.

Did you know
Cream and yoghurt pots make good slug traps when filled with milk or beer.

Grow potatoes in an old car tyre.
Increase your yield by neatly stacking up three or four tyres as the potato grows. This single tuber produced thirty-six potatoes in a single tyre.

Did you know
Silver foil and metal bottle tops make excellent bird scarers.

DO NOT DUMP IT – USE IT

Here are a few more ideas about how you can make use of other 'waste' items in your garden.

Net curtains These are useful as shading, frost protection and as carrotfly barriers

Bubble wrap This provides some frost protection

Ice-lolly sticks and strips cut from empty washing-up liquid bottles These can be used as plant labels.

Human hair and egg shells These are good for slug control

Bicycle inner tubes and old tights Cut into loops, these can be used as tree/plant ties

Corks Use as cane toppers

Polystyrene tiles and packaging Use large pieces to insulate compost bins and small bits as drainage in pots

Broken crockery Use this as drainage in pots

Car tyres These can be used as planters

Polystyrene boxes are ideal for seedlings as they provide extra warmth to the roots. Remember to pierce some drainage holes in the bottom

Make seed trays from plastic food boxes.

Pot on seedlings into cream, yoghurt pots etc. These can also be cut into strips and used as plant labels

Plastic water bottles make good mini greenhouses.

45

Old metal tins and watering cans can be transformed with simple paint techniques to create colourful flower pots.

A rusty old tin bath rejuvenated with painted decoration makes a wonderful fruit and vegetable container.

Apple juice cartons and some string can be recycled to form an attractive fruit bowl.

Index

Use some of your waste paper to make into pulp and
then create stunning aromatic paper and cards.

This version first published in Great Britain 1999

Search Press Limited
Wellwood, North Farm Road,
Tunbridge Wells, Kent TN2 3DR

in association with

The Henry Doubleday Research Association
National Centre for Organic Gardening
Ryton-on-Dunsmore
Coventry CV8 3LG

Reprinted 2000, 2002

The publishers and author can accept no legal
responsibilty for any consequences arising from the
information, advice or instructions given in this
publication.

The publishers would like to thank the following:

Claymore Grass Machinery, Bidford-on-Avon,
Warwickshire, for the loan of the machinery on pages 32
and 36 for photography.

Environmental Images, London, for the picture of the
landfill site at Great Wakering, Essex, on page 7.
© Robert Brook 1999.

Mathias Guepin, for all the helpful information about
composting in the tropics, and for the use of the
photographs on pages 26–27. © Mathias Guepin 1999.

The Irish Peatland Conservation Council for the use of the
photograph on page 7 showing moss peat extraction
from All Saints' Bog, Co. Offaly, Ireland. © Irish Peatland
Conservation Council 1999.

Donald MacIntyre, Countryside Advisor, Batheaston,
Bath, for the use of the of a wild meadow on page 35.
© Donald MacIntyre 1999.

George Morgan, of the Maidstone and District Allotments
Association, for providing the three photographs at the
top of page 14. © George Morgan 1999.

The idea for creating a compost bin from old car tyres,
shown on page 14, is based on the article, Tricks with
Tyres, by Dave Bevan, published in the March 1998
issue of *Organic Gardening* magazine.

The Recycle Works Ltd, Clitheroe, Lancashire, for the
photographs of the New Zealand box on page 15 and
the TigerWormery on page 28.

Sue Turner, head gardener at HDRA, Yalding, for help
and for sparing the time to pose for the compost making
pictures on pages 24–25.

Jackie and Martin Webb at the Mohair Centre,
Chiddingly, Sussex, for permission to roam round their
farm and take photographs.

Wiggly Wigglers Ltd., Lower Blakemere, Herefordshire,
for the supply of the graphic artwork for their 'Can
o'Worms' worm bin on page 29.

and John, Joyce, Tamsin and Ted for posing for
photography.

**The author would like to thank Bob
Crowder, who introduced her to Sir Albert
Howard; to Dick Kitto, who inspired her
compost making; and to Ned, who
activates it!**

Colour separation by P&W Graphics, Singapore
Printed in Spain by Elkar S. Coop. 48180 Loiu (Bizkaia)